The Stimulus Tragedy
And What You Can Do To Prevent It

By Branch Twigg

"Know well the condition of your flocks,
And pay attention to your herds;
For riches are not forever,
Nor does a crown endure to all
generations."

Proverbs 27: 23 – 24

The Stimulus Tragedy
And What You Can Do To Prevent It

By Branch Twigg

First Edition 2009

Manufactured in the United States of America

Branch Twigg, 2009
http://stimulustragedy.blogspot.com/

Editors: Branch Twigg and Bud Twigg

Publisher: L. F. Twigg

ISBN - 1442122544
EAN - 13 is 9781442122543

Dedication

This book is dedicated to the young, the worker and
small business owners. May you be all you can be!

About the Author

Branch Twigg resides in The United States of America. He has started, owned, operated and managed numerous businesses.

His biggest thrill is helping people be all they can be. He doesn't believe in competition in business. There is plenty of business to go around and he believes God gives him all he needs at all times. His belief is that every person has the power to be and have all they make up their mind to be and have. He believes he is blessed to have been born in this time and in this country. His ideal is to see The United States of America continue to be the greatest nation in the history of the world.

Foreword

WE THE PEOPLE are blessed to live in the greatest country the world has ever known. The Constitution and Bill of Rights, grant us the privilege to live free and elect people to preserve our principles and values. There are certain things that must be done and take place for this wonderful system to function properly and effectively. Sadly, these things are not being done. **WE THE PEOPLE** must wake up and take aggressive, positive and immediate action in order for our way of life to continue. The fact is we are losing ground in a big way and at a rapid pace.

Does that mean our way of life is already lost? Absolutely not! We are the greatest people living in the greatest nation ever. We have the opportunity, on a regular basis, to right any wrongs. I believe that **WE THE PEOPLE** will prevail, succeed and prosper, IF we wake up NOW! And I believe we will. The question is not whether we will survive, but rather, in what form. **Wake up Americans!**

"A house divided against itself cannot stand."

Abraham Lincoln

Contents

Introduction

As this writer has watched the events of the past several years, it has become more and more obvious that the trail we are on is taking us nowhere, fast. It seems that the solutions are clear, but no one is awake.

You might ask if I am a Democrat or a Republican. The answer to both is absolutely not! Both of our major political parties are badly broken. In fact, there is little hope for either of them as they exist today. They need complete restructuring. It is them or us.

The purpose of this book is to take an honest look at where the American people are and where we are likely to go. To explore the options and to recognize the solutions to the host of challenges this country faces. What America needs is good judgment and common sense. This is not an easy task when the politics of the aforementioned political parties are considered. The goal of this book is to simply examine the realities of the American situation in as few words as possible. The ideal of this project is to present **WE THE PEOPLE** with a wake up call in the hope that Americans will be motivated to take aggressive, positive and immediate action to heal our great nation.

United we stand, divided we fall.

"America will never be destroyed from the outside.
If we falter and lose our freedoms,
It will be because we destroyed ourselves."

Abraham Lincoln

Chapter 1

The Background

A government of **WE THE PEOPLE** will maintain itself and prosper only when disciplined.

This thought has been constantly on my mind in recent times. Americans have lost their discipline. This is a critical point and must be rectified, and the only way this can happen is from the bottom up.

It will never happen from the top down because we have no statesmen in government. At least there are not enough to make a difference.

What we have are politicians and blindly partisan politicians, at that. The rhetoric is there, but the actions prove that the moral and ethical principles are not. That is not to say there are no good people in government. In fact, there are many good people in government.

What is evident is these good people are blinded by partisan politics, don't have the back bone to stand up and do the right thing or are just not qualified to serve in the positions they've been elected to.

The power in politics today lies with entrenched, career politicians; many with personal agendas, and/or they have been bought off by special interests. They can be found in gross in both parties.

As long as **WE THE PEOPLE** continue to tolerate these entrenched, career politicians nothing will change; at least not for the better. Without term limits, which have been determined by the Supreme Court to be unconstitutional (U.S. Term Limits, Inc v. Thornton, 1995), the only way to remove these relics is to vote them out.

Why do we limit our Presidents to two terms and allow these Representatives and Senators to serve until they drop? It makes absolutely no sense.

So, Americans, remove these people after a reasonable amount of time. Twelve years in congress is long enough.

Career politicians get so twisted by special interests and trade offs that they cannot serve effectively for more than 12 years. And, it happens to all of them. This is one of the major reasons our country is in the mess it is in.

The federal government has an open checkbook.

No family, no worker, no small business will long survive without responsible spending. Our government has no restrictions. Politicians can spend whatever they choose to spend and they do.

Year after year, congress after congress, they continue to spend. On and on it goes – because **WE THE PEOPLE** allow it!

A wise old World War II vet told me many years ago "You can't spend yourself rich". The fact is the American voter allows these people to spend and spend and spend.

To make the situation worse, the President is feeding us fear bait. Don't take the bait.

"There is nothing to fear but fear itself"

**Franklin D. Roosevelt
1932**

As Americans we live in the greatest country the world has ever known.

We have a Constitution to protect and defend our country, preserve our freedoms and allow us to be all we can be.

Every American has the right to choose his or her way in work and play.

All of us have the freedom to travel freely from one end of the country to the other, unrestricted, by a variety of means.

Education is available to every one of us, either formally or informally.

We can work in whatever field we choose, in whatever part of the country we choose.

There is virtually no end to the opportunities available to each of us.

Sadly, this is all being threatened by entrenched politicians and self-interested individuals who believe they can run our lives better than we can.

I propose this is an evil that can be stopped and prevented. This book will explore what is happening and encourage you to take aggressive, positive and immediate action to correct an untenable situation in America.

You can be all you make up your mind to be, but only if you wake up, NOW!

"Anything important is never left to the vote of the people.
We only get to vote on some man;
We never get to vote on what he is to do."

Will Rogers

Chapter 2

The Entrenched

Who and what are "The Entrenched"?

One Webster definition of entrenched is:
"To place in a position of strength; establish firmly or solidly"

So, the entrenched then, are career politicians who are in a position of strength (power) and firmly in place.

The problem arises as a result of these entrenched, career politicians holding these offices so long they become owned and controlled by special interests.

What this inevitably results in are the special interest line-items that are attached to every bill. This becomes, and is, a matter of practice.

Someone writes a bill, and it may be a very good bill; then special interests jump on with line-items that become law as a part of a good bill. These line-items can be totally unrelated to the original bill, and most often are.

The entrenched manage to get support from their constituents for the original bill and the bill passes. Most voters don't even know the line-items are in the bill.

It becomes a game of political trade-offs. The entrenched say they will support the bill, but only if their special interest line-items are added to it.

WE THE PEOPLE have the power to stop this by voting these entrenched, career politicians out of office.

We cannot survive with America as it is and allow these relics to remain in office and continue to operate. So let's vote them out!

Some say many good politicians will be lost by doing this. That is certainly true in some cases. If the voters really like them, let them sit out for a term and rerun. Once they are out of office, much of their entrenched power is lost, and in order to restore it they will have to rebuild it. Mission accomplished. It will save our country.

Many of these politicians have been in office for 20 or more years. Ted Kennedy has been there for 46 years, Daniel Inouye, 46 years, Joe Biden was there for 36 years and Robert Byrd has been in office for 50 years, a record.

Research shows us what happens to the net worth of these entrenched, career politicians during their terms of office.

Many of them come in rich and leave richer. Those who don't come in with much, leave rich.

Where do they go once they're voted out? Most of them go to work for the companies they were responsible to regulate when in office, or become lobbyists for the same. A great many of them never leave Washington. After a couple of terms they don't remember how to get home.

For recent examples of how the entrenched operate and how closed this club is, review the Senate hearings for President Barack Obama's cabinet selections. At least five of them had tax problems surface at the hearings. One was appointed even with the tax problems.

Unbelievable! If any average American has similar tax problems, they go to jail! During one of the appointees hearing, Senators from both parties said "the Senate takes care of its own".

These people are the elected officials whom we send to Washington to manage our country. That's how it works. It needs to be broken up and it can't happen too soon.

The President must have line-item veto power, one way or the other.

This does two things. It keeps the entrenched from tacking these unrelated special interest line-items onto all bills, and it makes the President ultimately responsible to the people for any line-items that are allowed to pass.

The entrenched are very close to destroying themselves. All the Stimulus Packages will be exposed more and more over the next few years.

They will do little to stimulate anything, but the spending will go on for generations.

If **WE THE PEOPLE** will wake up, none of the entrenched voting for these free spending bills will remain in office. They must go.!

"I would rather go to bed without dinner than to rise in debt."

Benjamin Franklin

Chapter 3

Stimulus

What, exactly, is stimulus?

One Webster definition is:
"Something that incites or quickens action"

That is the definition that best fits what I understand the government is supposedly trying to do. The key word is "quicken."

What we are being told, and have been told since mid-2008 is that the US economy needs stimulus to "quickly" improve it.

So, in theory, if the government spends enough money they don't have, the economy will improve, 4 million jobs will be created and all will be well.

In late 2008 the government began to throw money, which they didn't have, at the US economy. Most of this money went to banks, which were all supposedly going to fail.

The banks proceeded to rat hole this money, go buy foreign banks and domestic banks, plan big Las Vegas parties and all sorts of other things that did nothing for anyone but the banks.

Little, if any, of this money hit the streets in the form of loans to businesses or individuals. To top this off, the money went to big banks as they were the ones with problems.

What you never hear about are all the thousands of small town banks across the country that were not in trouble and received no money. The small town banks are the ones that loan to small businesses and individuals and make the US economy work.

The big banks have no respect for **WE THE PEOPLE**. They should have been allowed to fail rather than profit from their misdeeds and then be rescued by the US taxpayer.

In 2009 the government, lead by the entrenched, will throw another $1 trillion at the US economy. Remember, they don't have this money!

What they aren't talking about is in addition to this $1 trillion is the interest that will be paid on it, and that assumes that the government can sell the debt.

In addition, there is an existing deficit. Add all these things together and it totals not $1 trillion, but more like $3 trillion and maybe even $3.5 trillion and many predictions now run as high as $15 trillion.

What are the details of the Stimulus Package? As a campaign promise, President Obama pledged that all bills would be published for review by, **WE THE PEOPLE,** for five days prior to his signing.

The entrenched then determined the Stimulus Package was "emergency spending" so it was not made available for our review online.

How about that! So how do we know what is in this monster Stimulus Package? The fact is, prior to signing, we did not.

Efforts made to get it published on independent web sites were unsuccessful and the way the review process was set up, the full measure will never be seen by **WE THE PEOPLE**.

The entrenched didn't want us to see it. There is so much garbage in the bill and so much that will not stimulate anything, that the entrenched didn't want us to see it.

Don't forget these, career, entrenched politicians really believe they are much smarter than **WE THE PEOPLE** and therefore what we don't know is for the best. They really believe this!

It is a spending bill from beginning to end. Most of the tax-reduction items were been taken out by the house, and the measure that would have limited the time that this bill would be in effect, to prevent it from becoming permanent spending, was defeated in the senate.

The fact is that very little of the Stimulus Package is actual stimulus. It is a progressive and permanent spending bill and very little of it will be spent in 2009. With that in mind, how does it stimulate anything? It doesn't! It won't!

Certainly there will be a portion of this money spent in 2009 and some of it will be stimulus. However, most of it, a high percentage, will not appear as 2009 spending and much of it will not appear until 2011 or later.

What do **WE THE PEOPLE** want our government to do?

A Rasmussen poll the last week of January 2009 said these things:

- 53% of Americans want tax cuts.
- 57% of Americans say that tax cuts generally help the economy.
- 43% of Americans would support an economic recovery plan that included only tax cuts and no new government spending.
- Only 27% of Americans say that the nation is heading in the right direction! (www.rasmussenreports.com)

With this information, why is our government spending? The fact is that the entrenched don't care what the voters think or want. They forget who sent them to Washington, who elected them and who they work for – and they don't care.

The arrogance is appalling. The saddest part of all is **WE THE PEOPLE** keep sending them back, term after term, to spend our money in any way they choose.

The entrenched have come to know **WE THE PEOPLE** will continue to send them back to Washington, term after term, and as a result have no concern about what **WE THE PEOPLE** really want or need.

This is the "Stimulus Tragedy". The Stimulus Package will not work. **WE THE PEOPLE** will be expected to pay for it and pay we will – for generations.

"Last year we said, "things can't go on like this" and they didn't, they got worse."

Will Rogers

Chapter 4

Trillion

How much is a trillion?

I heard recently that if you laid a $1,000 bill on the ground and piled enough of them on top of each other to equal a trillion dollars, that the stack would be 63 miles high.

So $3 trillion would be 189 miles of $1,000 bills. That's a lot of dough! And remember, we don't have it! Every trillion this insane government commits us to will cost every American $3300, or some say it will cost every head of household $80,000.00. And it increases every day with more and more free spending.

"Denial ain't just a river in Egypt."

Mark Twain

Chapter 5

Who Pays?

WE THE PEOPLE will pay. We will pay and pay and pay. President Obama was elected on the platform of change. However, he never disclosed what the change was to be. He also said 95% of Americans would get tax cuts. So why are there no substantial tax cuts in the Stimulus Package?

President Obama is in a tight spot. As a campaign promise he pledged that 95% of Americans would get a tax cut. His political success hinges on two things:

1)   a tax cut for 95% of Americans
2)   the success of the Stimulus Package

The challenge for the President is that those two things are in conflict with each other.

How is government going to finance the Stimulus Package and reduce taxes at the same time? It goes against everything we have seen during the first three months of 2009.

What has happened is the bill is plus or minus 30% temporary tax cuts and 70% spending. There has been no discussion regarding income tax cuts, which is what the voters are expecting.

In fact, all Americans are going to expect a tax cut in 2010. That is excluding those already in the top tax brackets and already paying a large part of income taxes collected in America.

I expect to see income tax cuts as the President gets further into his term. He will be reminded by the 53% of the voters who elected him that they must have income tax cuts. That really is not a big issue for the government to deal with. These income tax cuts will come in a very small way and he will be off the hook. The entrenched will tread very lightly in the area of income tax and income tax cuts. So, how will the Stimulus Package be paid for?

Taxes are going up and they are going up soon and fast! The government will come through the back door to raise taxes in many ways.

As the old saying goes "if you want to catch a horse thief, hire a horse thief to show you how to do it." Well, the government hired a horse thief in the Treasury Secretary, Timothy Geitner. He knows how to get around paying his taxes and he is now in charge of collecting ours.

We can be assured when we don't pay our taxes we will be persecuted and prosecuted, to the full extent of the law. Isn't that a fine deal? The fox is guarding the hen house. What a joke. Too bad it's not a funny joke. The government IS coming to take us away.

Those of us, who own small businesses, get pay checks from businesses or service businesses had better hold on tight. Small businesses, light industry, the worker and the family will have to pay for the Stimulus Package.

There is no one else to do it. Big business passes on its costs. It has to be the little guy who pays. It always has been and always will be. The only place any raw materials or basic services are produced is at the lowest level. Everything happens from the bottom up and never from the top down.

The President has said many times that "only government can fix the US economy." He is very, very wrong.

Only **WE THE PEOPLE** can fix the economy. Government spending only prolongs the misery. We as small business, the worker and the family will pay.

The big companies getting the welfare money aren't going to pay. They will pass their costs back to us. The entrenched are not going to pay. We have the reference of the Senate cabinet appointment hearings of 2009 to prove it.

The government can't pay – it doesn't have anything to pay with except our taxes or by printing funny money. What makes this so insidious is that the entrenched and the President are all lying to us.

They will begin, immediately, to tax us. Expect big tax increases on all "sin tax" items, such as booze and tobacco, etc. They will subsidize the core industries, with our tax monies, but we will pay more.

They will raise gasoline and fuel taxes, to pay for the "infrastructure improvements" set out in the Stimulus Package.

They won't begin building right away, it will take some time to strike a deal with a couple of the biggest construction companies (those giving the most to the entrenched in campaign donations, of course) and get them firmly in place so they make all the money. Local contractors won't have the "expertise" or "experience" to handle the job (not enough campaign contributions).

Then they will raise withholding taxes, social security taxes, and on and on and on. Oh, they won't raise individual income taxes for at least two years to fulfill campaign promises, but over time even that will change.

"I am prepared for the worst, but hope for the best."

Benjamin Desraeli
Prime Minister of the United Kingdom
In Office - 20 February 1874 – 21 April 1880

Chapter 6

Worst Case

The Stimulus Package has passed, along with several others, and the government says this is just the beginning. There are many other spending measures coming.

As long as **WE THE PEOPLE** do nothing, they will keep coming and coming. What we are being told is only part of the spending. There are costs related to administration and interest we haven't seen yet and the costs will continue to grow.

There will be very few new jobs created and most of these are years away. Any new jobs created by the Stimulus Package will disappear within 2 years.

The stock market will continue to move lower. The big money will short the market and it will plunge to lows that haven't been seen in decades. Small businesses will begin to fail and during the next two years, hundreds of thousands of small and mid-sized businesses will be shut down, costing millions more jobs.

Bankruptcies will be rampant. The stock market will continue to move lower and the nation will enter into a full-scale depression.

This disaster will spread worldwide and there will be no one to finance the runaway government spending. In order to finance the government debt, the presses will be running at capacity and the government will begin to print larger denomination bills.

Inflation will zoom upward to levels before unseen in America. The situation will greatly exceed what happened in the early 1980's.

The personal suffering will be unimaginable. Young families, the elderly and the poor will suffer the most. Social Security will go broke and all benefits will cease. Banks will fail in droves.

The entrenched, career politicians will continue to make all the wrong decisions. Government will take control of every aspect of our lives.

The housing industry will collapse. The transportation systems will collapse. The Second Amendment will be suspended and all guns will be confiscated in the name of the public good.

Once this is done, the government will suspend the First Amendment. Any public speeches will require a special permit issued by the government. There will be hundreds of thousands of political prisoners.

Anyone making any public speeches critical of the government will be locked up. Anything purchased will be with plastic cards with individual identification and pictures on them and these will be issued by the government at a cost to the user.

Since America is the driving force in the world it will cause a world economic collapse. The oil nations will sell no oil and those governments will collapse. Those that are strong enough to survive the initial devastation will be taken over by roaming nomads.

The poor countries of the world will see famine and millions of people will die. On and on and on it will go. It will be impossible to stop.

None of this has to happen and most likely it won't. To some degree, however, the wheels are already turning in that direction.

It is up to **WE THE PEOPLE** to stop it before it's too late.

"Man is not free unless government is limited."

Ronald Reagan

Chapter 7

Most Likely Scenario

As a result of the Stimulus Package, and all the other bills that have passed or have been proposed and will likely be passed, the wheels are in motion.

In order to meet his campaign promise of 95% of the people receiving tax cuts, it will have to be done. They will be small, insignificant income tax cuts or tax credits. The reality is no one will really contribute any less to the government.

Any tax cuts received will be taken back when the next tax return is filed or it will be collected in some other way.

It is not yet clear how they will do that, but the government has no intention of giving anyone a real tax cut.

Within two years there will be no sign of any tax cuts, but the government will continue to talk about them even though they don't exist.

The primary goal will be to make people think that 95% of Americans are getting a tax cut in order to strengthen the majority in Congress at the mid-term elections in 2010.

It is assumed that **WE THE PEOPLE** are not bright enough to figure out what is happening before the third year. By then enough of these Stimulus Packages and the government's agenda will be firmly in place. They hope, and may be right, the press and the people will still be caught up in the euphoria of the 2008 elections to carry their agenda through the mid-term elections.

As all this is happening, the back door to taxation will be opened. In fact, it has already been opened. Tax increases are already taking place!

On the premise of "making the rich pay their fair share" a host of tax increases are being implemented. Sadly, these taxes are attacking those citizens who already pay the bulk of taxes in this country. Don't believe for an instant that 95% of the people are paying the majority of the taxes in this country.

The fact is that about 5% of the people pay most of the taxes. We have been told the "rich" don't pay their fair share, but the reality is the highest earners pay most of the taxes in this country. These taxpayers include hundreds of thousands of small businesses that are the employers of the American worker.

Millions upon millions of Americans are now under attack. Go up and down the streets of your town and count all the small businesses that line the street. For every major factory or industry there are thousands of small businesses. Under this administration most of them fit the category of "rich" and they are going to pay more taxes, increasing their cost of doing business.

When the government overtaxes the producers of America they stop producing. When the cost of doing business becomes so high that there is no longer profit in it, the incentive to produce is destroyed.

Anyone with money is becoming afraid to spend it. They are hedging against this spending by shorting the stock market and holding onto their cash. They will continue to hold it or invest it out of the country until the spending stops and their security is no longer at risk.

Increased taxation stops investment at all levels. The big money stops spending, then small business followed by individuals.

Let me ask a few questions. Are you buying anything? Are you spending any money for anything you don't absolutely need?

I already know the answers. No one is spending anything because they are afraid of the economy, and if no one spends, the economy continues to worsen. If the individual stops buying goods and services, the economy is depressed.

Everything has to flow up from the bottom. That is all but one thing. When taxes are raised on the producers, which include small business and the individuals with substantial capital, they stop investing in business. Then people lose jobs, and that is us, and then we have no money with which to buy goods and services. That is why the stock market has reacted so negatively to what the government is doing.

The spending the government is doing is an attempt to push money down and make the economy better. This theory never works because there is no incentive for the producers to produce and thereby no money flowing to us at the base level with which we buy goods and services.

The administration elected in 2008 has opened the back door to all sorts of new taxes. Capital gains tax rates are going up, which is a huge hit to the producers. Also, the base tax rates to the producers are going up. Both of these are going up with no end in sight. Many of them will not survive it.

Just these two tax increases alone will stop production. But that is just the beginning and we need to pay attention.

Sin taxes, on products such as tobacco and alcohol have already been proposed. Federal withholding taxes and self- employment taxes are next. There will be taxes on everything imaginable, if we allow it.

The government will raise gas and fuel taxes, set up user fees on everything from roads to airports. There will be taxes proposed on the internet. National sales taxes will be proposed.

Rationing will be proposed on such things as gas and oil and taxes will be added to the cost at that time. More Social Security and Medicare costs will be passed on to the user. Social Security will eventually collapse and Medicare will go with it.

Following closely behind tax increases comes inflation. Regardless of what happens inflation will be a reality. There is no way all this new spending can be financed. There is no one to buy the debt. The only way the spending can be financed is to print massive amounts of new currency. That is already taking place.

We can be assured that the presses are running at maximum capacity to have huge amounts of new currency ready to be pushed on the people at a moments notice.

To add to all this misery, the IRS is coming for us. We are an easy mark. The government needs our money and will go to any length to get it. We are the easiest way, the shortest distance between two points.

WE THE PEOPLE don't have the time, the energy or resources to fight them and they will be relentless. Ask anyone who has been through it. There are many. It is a horrific experience. Since the entrenched, career politicians – and the cabinet member in charge of the IRS – don't have to pay their taxes that just leaves **WE THE PEOPLE**. Prepare yourselves. There is a double standard and you are the losing double.

All this will get as bad as the voter allows it to get. Some of it has already happened. We are too far down the trail now to stop it, but it doesn't have to go full circle. The American voters control how bad this situation gets.

Become active and stop it, NOW!

"I'm not a real movie star. I've still got the same wife
I started out with twenty eight years ago."

Will Rogers

Chapter 8

Media and Hollywood

Beware the media! Virtually everything we see or hear on the news is slanted. The entrenched control the media. The only thing we will hear and see is what they want us to hear and see.

If we get all our news from the major networks we're not getting anything other than what they want us to get. Print is just as bad and in many cases worse. At least with print media we can pick and choose which articles and writers we want to read and thereby sort out some of the garbage.

I know many successful and intelligent people who rarely, if ever, watch network television news. For them it is poison. They understand slanted news is not good for them, and it puts them in a position to pick up on negativity. They won't allow that to happen.

This author rarely watches any of the major networks including ABC, CBS or NBC. In fact, I read a regional paper online and rarely anything else and I pass on any articles that are not of interest. I sort the news. That helps me to stay in a positive mental state.

Beware the enlightened! These are the intellectual and celebrity types who believe they are smarter than us by virtue of their education or gifted abilities. Or just because of their money, which they happened to pick up from us and our support of them.

They often have great gifts of God-given talents. Their conceit emanates from them. They are prone to bash everything and everyone who doesn't think as they do or has less than they have.

They forget where they came from or how they got where they are. They travel around the world, trading love partners at every stop; often talking down America, meeting with dictators, despots, terrorists and all sorts of unsavory characters and enemies to America. It is often treasonous. They make such obscene amounts of money, thanks to us, that they really don't care about taxes or the cost of living, or the cost of anything. They totally lose touch with reality because they live in a fairy-tale world.

Look at this example. If you had $1 million and the tax rate was 50%, could you live decently and survive on $500,000? Of course you could.

More realistically, however, is that you earn $60,000, with two of you working and you pay 50% in taxes. Can you live decently and survive on $30,000? Not very well.

You need two cars so you can both work. You have children, insurance, house payments and on and on and on.

Life is a struggle to say the least. But you are grateful for what you have, your country and your freedom.

Now, we have to sort this crowd. This is about those who make all the noise and money and do little but disgrace America. It is impossible for these people to relate to us. They have lost touch with good or gratitude or God and I feel sorry for them.

Sadly, they are in front of our children all the time. The major networks put them on display as though they were really something special when in reality they are to be pitied and prayed for. Pay no attention to them, don't support them and, yes pray for them. They are misguided souls and nothing more.

Hopefully, our children will eventually see them for what they really are, lost souls.

This discussion is not about all those who do and have given so much. Praise these and pay no mind to the others.

"People seem not to see that their opinion of the world is also a confession of character."

Ralph Waldo Emerson

Chapter 9

Bashing

As a follow up to the last chapter, it is very unnerving to see the media, the entrenched and special interests bashing our great country.

For instance, we have the greatest military the world has ever seen. These people are volunteers and they do what they are asked to do very well.

Since Afghanistan began I have seen the media, the entrenched, many of these Hollywood types and intellectuals openly critical and disrespectful of our military personnel. Your military doesn't start wars, they finish them. The entrenched start wars.

Every person in America has a responsibility to support our military personnel and treat them as the preservers of our way of life, as people and with respect. Of particular concern is when the top dog in the US Senate, Harry Reid, a Democrat from Nevada, tells the world the cause is lost when we have troops in the field. It is treasonous. This has happened over and over and over again. Well, I say "Mr. Reid you must go and the sooner the better"!

Our military personnel deserve better.

All my life I have watched people become all they could be and rise to the top. A few of them have become Presidents of the United States of America. They deserve much better then they get – all of them.

I don't agree with many of them or all that has been done by any of them. But they are our President's and they deserve our respect. We can agree to disagree, respectfully.

Please don't participate in the bashing of our leaders in a disrespectful way. We degrade only ourselves when we do, and it is un-American.

There may be no one alive who disagrees more strongly with the policies of President Obama than me. But, that said, I respect his ability to press his point, state his case and carry through with his objectives. He is a successful person and deserves the respect of every American for it.

"All men having power ought to be distrusted to a certain degree."

James Madison

Chapter 10

Who Runs America?

There are an estimated 304,000,000 people in the United States of America. Approximately 218,000,000 are over eighteen. 169,000,000 were registered to vote in the 2008 election. 86,000,000 were determined to be Democrat, 55,000,000 Republican and 28,000,000 were registered as other.

That is a lot of voting power. It is interesting that 49,000,000 Americans choose not to register to vote, so at least that many have no say in how the government is operated.

I know quite a few of these non-voters and they all have the same reason for not voting, "it doesn't matter, my vote won't make any difference." Of course, I don't understand that line of thinking. Obviously that is untrue. The unregistered, non-voters have enough power to change the outcome of any election!

So, who is responsible for operating the government for **WE THE PEOPLE**? We are! All citizens eligible to vote are responsible. What we do then, is elect other citizens to represent us and in theory, manage our government. Let's take a look at how this works.

There are 535 Senators and Congressmen – 100 Senators (two from each state) and 435 congressmen. Also, you have an elected President and nine Supreme Court Justices, which are appointed by the President.

Even though the President is considered the most powerful person in the world his powers are limited under the constitution. The President has many discretionary powers. However, without congress behind him it can be very difficult for him to get anything done.

The fact is that congress has the power. Those 535 people are charged with running our country. Ideally, the Supreme Court keeps them from destroying our Constitution, which they seem to be in a hurry to do.

Sadly, the Congress is controlled by the entrenched. That needs to change, but as of today the entrenched are in complete control.

The first thing **WE THE PEOPLE** must do to regain control of the government and stop the insanity of this free spending of our money, is to vote out every Congressman or Senator who has been in office more than 12 years.

That means the voters are responsible for recruiting replacements who put their oath of office in upholding the Constitution first, above all else.

The second thing we must do is elect a President who has the courage and integrity to initiate a Line-Item Veto. That means every bill is scrutinized for special interest line-items added to bills, and if they are there, veto the bill and send it back to the Congress.

To get to the point of this chapter it is necessary to revisit the Line-Item Veto, which was declared unconstitutional (Clinton v. City of New York, 1998).

The purpose of the Line-Item Veto was to give the President the power to veto special interest provisions in any bill presented to the President for signing.

There is no need to debate the fact that the Line-Item Veto does not exist.

However, I would say that the Line-Item Veto places a huge responsibility on the President to do the right thing and not allow a mass of special interest line-items on any bill. This would save a ton of money for the taxpayer and help keep everyone in federal government honest.

This process would soon begin to weed out a lot of the special interest trash that gets stuck into bills and make the Congress accountable.

It will take a President with courage, fortitude, honor, ethics and a strong sense of values to do this. Can we find such a person? I believe we can, if we look in the right places.

They are not to be found in the halls of Congress. It will have to be an outsider with no political paybacks to be concerned with, someone with a thick skin and a clean heart.

I say, lets find this person and save our country!

"There is nothing wrong with America that faith, love of freedom, intelligence and energy of her citizens cannot cure."

Dwight D. Eisenhower

Chapter 11

The Illegal Aliens

The most serious challenge facing America is the issue of the illegal aliens in the country. You might ask why I consider this to be the most serious challenge. When I finish this chapter I hope you know why this is and why it is so important to address this immediately.

I will first surprise you with this point. The issue of lost jobs is the least important point of the illegal alien issue.

Why would I say something like that? Because the illegal aliens in this country include some of the most industrious people there are in the world.

Think of it this way. How many Americans would be willing to work at intensely hard jobs, for less pay in many cases, than the person working next to them?

How many Americans would be willing to live like most of these illegal aliens live and then send 80% of their earnings home to care for their families, or even live hundreds or thousands of miles away from their families to take the jobs they have?

Those are just two of the sacrifices many of these people make. America is dependent on these workers. Your economy will no longer function well without them.

The challenge of the having the illegal alien in America is not the lost jobs. I would bet if we removed all the illegal aliens from America today, there would be an instantly serious economic impact.

I also believe if we then offered all those jobs to Americans who were unemployed the positions would be difficult to fill.

Even today with high rates of unemployment these jobs would be difficult to fill. Americans won't work that hard for those wages. With those points in mind we can then look at all the other aspects of the illegal alien.

It is estimated, in conservative numbers, that there are plus or minus 20,000,000 illegal aliens in America. Those numbers are more likely in the range of 30,000,000 to 40,000,000. Now we are getting into the discussion that really matters when talking about illegal aliens.

It is generally assumed that these people are Mexican. For geographical reasons, they make up the large majority, but the reality is these people come from all over the world.

If only 5% of them are engaged in criminal activities, that number would be in the range of 1,000,000 to 2,000,000.

That is a huge number of bad actors who are testing America's law enforcement, court and prison resources. But even this is not the major impact of the illegal alien.

The number one problem with regard to the illegal alien is how it stretches the resources of services, medical and educational systems.

Because there is no record of these people, the number is impossible to calculate. Conservative estimates run from $30,000,000,000 to $45,000,000,000 and a more realistic number is likely closer to $100,000,000,000 annually. Yes, that is billions.

Some of the costs are related to education, welfare, medical, law enforcement, local and state government and many more. The positive impact as wage earners is not nearly as large a factor as the negative costs related to services.

That is because, for the most part, illegal aliens don't pay income taxes and they don't buy goods and services because they send their money home.

Every year these numbers go up dramatically as more and more of these people flow into the United States. Statistics show that fewer and fewer of them ever leave. Verification to support this information is readily available from many sources online.

The second most serious point of this is the impact on national security. As it now stands, there is no way to protect the Mexican border. There are not enough law enforcement personnel to even begin to stop the flow into the country.

It is only a matter of time before a major criminal or terrorist event occurs in America that is traced back to this open border. As this book is being written the drug gangs are entering the southern Border States and kidnapping and murdering. Citizens in all the Border States are in great peril.

Then there is the drug traffic, which is the most press worthy of the news we hear. This is a huge business, much bigger than anyone knows. With it comes the unsavory element in the form of illegal aliens who are required to distribute and intimidate.

All sorts of the worst capital crimes are a part of it. Then it begins to cost huge sums of money to enforce the law, go to trial and fill up the prisons with a most unsavory lot.

The entrenched know that America is spending unbelievable sums of money to support the illegal aliens. They don't want to deal with it because of the economic impact of deporting these people and having to fill these jobs with higher priced American workers.

Special interests, namely business, do not want to lose the illegal alien worker. Because the entrenched are so bought up after years of receiving campaign contributions and kickbacks from the employers, the situation just rolls on and gets bigger year by year.

Remember that millions of these illegal aliens are hired at minimum wage or less and business needs them to maintain profits. That is why this situation is not addressed.

Replace the entrenched, career politicians and this situation would soon be solved in a sensible, fair and humane way.

There is a solution. America needs to make securing the Mexican border a number one priority. This would be a true stimulus project in many ways.

First, securing the border stops the influx of the illegal aliens.

Second, it keeps our people safe.

Third, it stops the acceleration of costs at the federal, state and local levels.

Fourth, it saves government enough to go a long way toward fiscal responsibility and a balanced budget.

Now then, to actually securing the border. This country has a US Army Corps of Engineers. These people have accomplished many jobs much tougher than this one.

Call in the Army and the Corps of Engineers. The Army can patrol to keep the Corps and contractors safe and fence that border, every inch of it and do it right.

Start at each end of the border and charge toward the middle. The border can be divided into segments and bid by independent contractors. No contractor will receive more than two segments. The Corps of Engineers will design and manage the project. It is no small task but it can and must be done, NOW!

There is no need to deport mass numbers of illegal aliens. In fact it is not a practical solution. What needs to be done is to begin now to register all illegal aliens, issue picture identification cards and Social Security numbers.

Make clear to the illegal aliens that all law abiding, productive working people will be allowed to stay, work and pay taxes like every other American. In the process of this the criminal element will begin to be located and deported. By the time the border is secured, those people wanting to stay and become productive Americans will be well on their way.

As part of the border fence will be four deportation points. One in the far east area, one in the far west and two in the middle. These can be constructed a mile or so on the American side of the border on federal lands. These facilities will be a processing point for deportations of any illegal aliens not registered at the time of the completion of the fence.

The deportees will arrive at these facilities by bus and sent back to Mexico in a humane and considerate way. These points can also be developed into security points and camps for military personnel who will patrol the border.

In order to keep the border secure, the Army will patrol it in the air and on the ground and with electronics and cameras. The country is safe.

The law enforcement agencies can then begin to break up the drug runners and round up the gangs and get them out of the country. At the same time any illegal aliens in prison for anything other than capital crimes can also be deported.

There will be no safe-haven states or localities. If any states or localities are found to be harboring illegal aliens they can be prosecuted for obstructing justice and lose federal funding.

Over a period of 5 years or less the problem of the illegal alien will be a thing of the past. The federal government will have generated true stimulus in numerous ways. Over $100 billion dollars annually will be saved by federal, state and local governments.

The workers left in America will become productive citizens and pay taxes and billions more will be generated as tax revenues. The government can implement sensible immigration policies to allow productive people to immigrate as it always has.

For this to work all the insane ideas currently being proposed in the Amnesty Bill must be set aside. Here we go again. Remove the entrenched, career politicians and this challenge will be soon solved.

The American people will agree to do the right thing. They will not agree to giving illegal aliens a great home and all sorts of special interest handouts with it. Forget the nonsense. This is a simple, common sense and practical solution to a very serious challenge facing America. It is humane and moral.

The immigrant has made this country great and that can continue as it always has.

"You can always count on America to do the right thing – after they've tried everything else."

Winston Churchill

Chapter 12

Mexico

The most serious security challenges in America will come from Mexico. Terrorism can take many forms and Mexico is the doorway for terrorists.

We already have 2,000,000 or more illegal criminals and terrorists here in the form of illegal aliens and many more are coming. The worst and most deadly terrorist acts will come by way of Mexico during the next several years. It is inevitable.

The most fearsome of terrorists may be the drug runners and the drug cartels of Mexico. This problem is already spilling over into America and the entrenched are doing nothing about it.

Illegal firearms are moving in huge volumes into the United States through the Mexican border to support the drug runners. Law enforcement is dramatically outgunned.

It's only a matter of time before these drug runners are consolidated enough to create war on a large scale all across the United States.

The fact is the drug runners can afford more and better firearms than our law enforcement agencies have access to. Tie that to gang participation for the purpose of distributing the drugs and it is only a matter of time before there are heavily armed gangs terrorizing the entire nation. This could happen at any moment. Northern Mexico is totally out of control.

This open border presents the perfect means for all sorts of terrorists to gain access to the United States.

The next 9/11 will most likely come from terrorists crossing the Mexican border. Wake up America! Fence that border! Every inch of it, NOW!

"An unlimited power to tax involves, necessarily, the power to destroy."

Daniel Webster

Chapter 13

Tax Increases

The success or failure of this country is going to hinge on tax policy. It is important to examine tax as a cost to America.

For the entrenched, it is the means to achieve their end. Without tax revenues their agenda fails and that is exactly what must happen – they must fail.

If what is going on in America continues as it is, the entrenched will control the country and that is socialism. All things considered that is the ultimate goal.

Remember the entrenched believe **WE THE PEOPLE** are not intelligent enough to manage our own lives. They believe that only they have the answers. That only they can do the best for the people. That we need them for everything and without them we are a hopeless lot.

As long as these entrenched, career politicians remain in office, this will be the case. They write and approve all Stimulus Packages and in order to fund them they must tax **WE THE PEOPLE**.

There are so many aspects to the IRS tax code that no one could possible know all of it. If you get a copy of it, which you can, it is something like 17,000 pages long. It is so complicated, involved and ever changing that it is nearly impossible to follow, track or comprehend.

The entrenched want it that way. It is much easier for these people, who consider themselves smarter than us, to slip and sneak money away from us this way. Taxes are an ever growing sore on our country. For **WE THE PEOPLE** they are a death sentence.

Every time the entrenched pass any bill it costs us money. Every time a bill is passed it is assumed that we will pay for it. In fact we are demanded to pay for it.

One way or another, in every case, we must pay for it. Manufacturers will try to pass tax costs on to us in the form of higher prices in the market place. Service companies raise the cost of services. On and on it goes, but we always pay.

The entrenched have gone to great lengths to convince us that **WE THE PEOPLE**, 95% of us, will receive a tax cut. What they are going to do is to give most of the people a small income tax cut. That is for everyone except "The Rich".

They believe that we are too ignorant to realize this is not possible. There is no way that spending can be funded unless we pay. They have told us "The Rich" are going to pay for it; they are going to finally pay their fair share.

The fact is the truly affluent already pay most of the tax. If they can convince the general public "The Rich" are bad guys and they deserve to pay, it enables them to fulfill their agenda, which is to make the majority of the people dependent on them.

This is a life work and a mission for these people. Everyone must wake up and understand this is not being done for you; it is being done for them and their agenda. The easiest way to control us is to keep us broke and always struggling to make ends meet.

Taxes are the easiest way for them to do that. And all the while this is happening they promise tax cuts and it sounds really great to people. It is a lie.

The Obama tax cut promise that was largely responsible for him being elected was a lie, pure and simple. Hopefully, the country will awaken and stop all this nonsense before it too late.

Here is a suggestion. Ask your tax accountant to explain what happens to any tax cut, or refund money you have been promised. If you really get it, and if it is money you can actually keep, I will be surprised.

In some way you will be taxed on it or in some manner will be forced to give it back

It always works this way. It always has and always will unless **WE THE PEOPLE** stop it. The reality is, when all is said and done, we will pay more taxes and in ways we have never imagined.

When discussing taxes and a sound economy it is necessary to realize income and profits always come from the bottom and flow upward, and it never works to push them down from the top. That is why all this spending is so insidious.

The government is trying to push money down through spending. There are few benefits to be realized by using this approach.

Something has to be created to generate income and thereby profits that can be taxed. Creation has to come from some sort of basic, renewable source to be real, permanent and beneficial.

In the good old days, if there has ever been such a time, this was agriculture, forestry, mining and things like that. These days, in the technological age, there is little real, permanent and beneficial growth.

That is the reason for crashes such as the technology meltdown a few years ago and the devastating effects of this mortgage crisis. There was nothing real, permanent and beneficial being created or produced because all that was being created was debt and speculation.

It doesn't take much to tip all that over, and over time it always gets top heavy and tips over. There are only so many profits to take from the root base. It is all speculation based on greed. If this were not true, we wouldn't be seeing all these big investment scams of recent times. Sadly, greed will take over again in a few years and many people will get to go through all this again.

The base of any economy has to have roots in creating at a basic level to have any long term stability. That basic level is agriculture, forestry, mining, oil production and things of that nature. Small business is the natural vehicle that develops and begins the marketing of these things. Small business drives the economy. Everything of value starts there. It always has and always will.

Profitable small business begins the flow from the base level. So as we talk about taxes we have to start the process from the small business level. There are millions of small businesses in this country and they are your life blood. They are the ones that are going to suffer the most in the Stimulus Tragedy.

The new President has picked an arbitrary number of $250,000 and all earners over that are determined to be "rich" and are considered to be fair game for tax increases. The problem with this is this number includes millions of the base economic producers in America. This will be devastating to the economy.

In order to explain why it is necessary to examine who falls into this earning category. Included in this $250,000 number are most people involved in the base producing industries such as agriculture, forestry, etc. In fact there are millions of main street small businesses all across America that are now considered "rich."

These are the same people who do most of the hiring. There are many more people employed by small business, the "New Rich", than by big business. In most families, where the husband and wife both work, one or both of them are employed by small business.

Keep in mind we are talking about the base producers, the beginning point of the economy. To increase taxes on these businesses is going to directly affect how many employees they have, how much expansion they do and how much risk they are willing to take.

Many of these businesses are already scaling down their businesses to stay under the $250,000 limit. We will see many businesses decide to scale down rather than go over the limit and pay more tax. Small businesses cannot spend more than they earn. They are not entrenched politicians. They must budget and operate responsibly. They will be hurt the most and at the same time they hold America's greatest hope.

So, small business is hurt first by tax increases. Second is the worker, who is the employee of small business. Third, and most critical, is the family. Parents losing small business jobs will result in millions of families being forced to live on one income, or with no jobs or income at all.

It is already happening as a result of this insane spending spree of the entrenched and increased taxes will make it much worse. Businesses, workers and families are not spending. This is the base level. I know of no one buying anything they don't have to have. Parents will give what they can in an effort to keep their children as safe and secure as possible. At some point, with no jobs, basic things must be cut. That deepens the cycle, and the economy continues to worsen.

Tax increases on business are a very negative thing. Business is required to pay for most of everything already. Anytime the entrenched enact any law, it is always business that is forced to pay first.

Business is already spending too much time, resources and money meeting the requirements of government. It is discouraging, as a business operator, to see employees working endlessly on government reports, withholding statements, payroll reports, licensing, unemployment documentation, bonding reports, insurance issues and many, many more production killers. It is an endless cycle of nonproductive time, resources and money.

Now these hard working, producing businesses have been determined to be "rich" and need to be persecuted with more taxes. What needs to happen to get the economy moving forward again is to remove government burdens, not add to them. Tax increases on business is the second worst thing for the economy, behind only spending.

About the real rich. These are the 5% or so of Americans who are always under attack by the entrenched. They are the bad guys. At least that is what we are always told.

This is the most disgusting thing any sensible person has ever heard. This country was founded by good people, immigrants, looking for religious freedom and opportunity to be all they could be.

The American Constitution was written in such a way that all Americans could become all they had the goals, guts and determination to achieve. It grieves me to see the entrenched try so hard to destroy all initiative for individuals to reach out and be all they can be.

As I think about how to write this portion of the chapter, I remind you that you have the opportunity to be as successful and wealthy as you choose to be. There is no country in the world that offers as much to the individual as America does. That is why you are here!

Unless you are a Native American, you are descendents of immigrants. Your roots go back to immigrants who came here for freedom and opportunity. Certainly there were immigrants who came to America with fortunes, but the vast majority came with nothing.

Most of the rich are beneficiary of successes that were made in America. Fortunes are seldom made by luck, theft or dishonest means.

Ingenuity, imagination, courage, determination and tenacity have made most of the fortunes in America. The wealthy of America are not the bad guys; they are the innovators and capital providers of America.

Tax and persecute the affluent in America and the flow of capital stops flowing. This immediately impacts small business, then every worker, family and parent in the country.

The affluent have many options. They can invest their money in other countries or just sit on it. What we are seeing now is that a lot of money from the affluent is flowing into raw land as a place to invest it with minimal risk while waiting for the economy to improve and as a hedge against inflation. When the economy does improve this money will begin to flow again. If this money leaves the country it does nothing for America.

The United States cannot afford to raise taxes on the affluent. In fact, for the economy to recover and prosper we must lower taxes, especially on the affluent and the "New Rich". The country needs that capital to promote small business which drives the economy from the bottom up.

"Where is the politician who has not promised to fight to the death for lower taxes who has not proceeded to vote for the very spending projects that make tax cuts impossible?"

Barry Goldwater

Chapter 14

The Tax Solution

Unless the insane policy of free spending and tax increases is reversed America is headed for a full scale depression. It is inevitable.

The course we are on is economic suicide. Here is how to stop the economic decline. There are several things to be done to jump start the economy, stop the stock market crash and instantly recover a healthy economy.

Immediately stop all tax on capital gains. This is the fastest and surest way to get the affluent to reinvest in the country. Business of all types will respond and become excited about the future. The stock market will stop free falling.

This is true stimulus.

Cease all forms of inheritance taxes. There are millions of people in business at the base level who are of an age to retire. The present tax system double taxes the life work of these people and many of them will lose the gains of their life work to taxes. It is criminal.

I believe this move would be extremely beneficial in many ways. Rather than forcing many businesses to close because of this tax, the businesses would be passed on to family and keep producing. Even if the inheritance was passed to heirs outside the business it would keep producing.

When inheritance taxes are paid, it goes to the entrenched and is gone forever. When passed to heirs with no tax it continues to produce and generate more tax revenues. Inheritance taxes are the most unfair tax of all and why **WE THE PEOPLE** have allowed them at all is a sad story.

This is true stimulus.

Instead of persecuting small business there must be a consistent, never changing policy of income averaging. Business cycles go up and down in the best of times and income averaging can make all the difference whether or not a business can function year by year.

Just knowing there is a consistent and never changing policy of income averaging will stimulate the economy and enable small business to secure required operational financing.

This is true stimulus.

For all married couples with children, declare a three-year moratorium on all federal taxes for incomes less than $50,000, effective for the 2009 tax year. Then do the same for married couples with no children with incomes less than $40,000 and the same for singles with incomes less than $20,000.

This will create the optimism to get people to loosen up and begin buying goods and services again. It is measurable by both the taxpayer and the government, costs less than these multi-billion dollar Stimulus Packages and entails no oversight to prevent corruption.

It also solves the health care problem by allowing families to purchase health insurance. Try it for three years and if it doesn't work it can be changed. But it will work and it makes sense. These people generate a small portion of the total tax revenues anyway, but it is a lot of money to them.

This is true stimulus.

These tax changes will heal the country within 2 years, IF the entrenched are removed from office and replaced with responsible Americans so the spending can be stopped. Permanently applying these changes will keep optimism flowing and the economy producing.

We don't need more taxes. We need less spending. Couple lower taxes with responsible spending and the economy heals very fast.

This is true stimulus.

Remove the entrenched, career politicians from office. Make responsible spending a reality. Establish these tax changes permanently. And watch these positive changes grow into a permanently healthy economy.

America could then function perfectly well with a 15 to 20 percent flat tax rate and still exclude the lower income earners.

"Don't gamble; take all your savings and buy some good stock and hold it till it goes up, and then sell it. If it don't go up, don't buy it!"

Will Rogers

Chapter 15

Stock Market

The stock market has crashed and at the time of this writing continues to fall on almost a daily basis. This is a predictable result of undisciplined spending, promises of continued undisciplined spending and tax increases. The smart money will short the market. As long as this wild spending continues that position will be the dominant thinking. Until the market finds a solid bottom this will not and cannot change.

How low will the stock market go? There is no limit to where this could go. Unless there is aggressive, positive and immediate action taken by **WE THE PEOPLE** the stock market could continue until it is essentially worthless! Many experts believe the low could be less than 3000.

We have seen nothing yet compared to how bad the economy could get if this insane spending is not stopped. It may be too late to stop the free fall. The current administration continues to tell us the spending must continue and almost daily announces more spending programs. There is no confidence in the market by anyone with any common sense.

The next generation of Billionaires is being created at this moment. Those investors having the foresight to short the market are making millions every day. There is no reason for them to change their positions until a firm bottom is established and there is no bottom in sight. Any upswings prior to the establishment of that bottom will be profit taking, which makes good sense.

Until the mid term elections the entrenched, career politicians will be in control of government.

That means nothing can permanently change until these free spenders are replaced. It means the only thing **WE THE PEOPLE** can do is become very vocal.

Every American must contact their Representatives and Senators and tell them if they don't cease and desist this spending you will vote them out of office.

Should this stock market free fall continue the results may be irreconcilable. Please America, make that call, send that fax or email and make it a point to repeat the process daily. Our freedom depends on it!

"Beware of little expenses. A small leak will sink a great ship."

Benjamin Franklin

Chapter 16

Spending

Government spending is a cancer on this economy and every economy. Every dollar the government spends must come out of our pocket. One way or another, we will pay. That means every dollar the government spends is at least one dollar we won't have.

The entrenched have worked hard since the 1930's to convince **WE THE PEOPLE** that we get back more than we pay in. The fact is we never get it back. Our Representatives and Senators go to great lengths to convince us they are our benefactors, our friends and our saviors. These are lies.

Whatever we get from them comes at a price, some today and some tomorrow. From this point forward it is multi-generational spending. The spending taking place in 2009 will require multiple generations to pay for it. And, year by year it will get worse due to compounding. This is debt and debt carries interest.

Why can't **WE THE PEOPLE** understand what is happening? Does the public believe they will get more than they pay? Does the public believe these entrenched politicians know what is best for them? Or is the public so apathetic they just don't care?

It is obviously a combination of each of these. The entrenched don't care what answer it is with us, just so long as we do nothing and let them continue to take over and destroy our freedom and our lives. That is what they want!

This is not about just spending. They know that if they can get complete control of us through insane spending, tax increases and legislating our freedoms away they will own us and our children for all time. That is what they want!

Always remember they truly believe we can't live without them and that are much smarter than we are.

Wake up and save our country!

"I love to go to Washington –if only to be near my money."

Bob Hope

Chapter 17

Government Income

The entrenched get most of their money from taxes. **WE THE PEOPLE** pay taxes so they can spend us into oblivion and thereby control our lives.

There is another way and America must replace these entrenched, career politicians so these things can happen. They are simple, effective and just make good sense.

There are millions of acres of government owned land in the United States. Every effort must be made to harvest the resources available as a part of these lands. These efforts must be made in a responsible manner with common sense environmental attention applied to each.

Harvesting unused and wasted resources is in the best interest of **WE THE PEOPLE**. Revenues generated to the government cost the public nothing, replace needed tax dollars and create real jobs. The country needs these resources to be harvested and turned into cash to heal the economy and pay off debt.

This is true stimulus.

The United States Forest Service controls millions of acres of prime un-harvested timber. Each year we watch millions of acres of this timber burned in forest fires. That is an unconscionable waste. Whatever timber can be harvested must be harvested. This does not mean clear cutting. It means harvesting prime timber in a responsible way. This timber is contracted by business and it generates immediate revenues.

Oil in the ground generates no revenues. America is not acting in a rational manner with regard to domestic oil production. Every effort needs to be made to develop all available domestic oil resources. This needs to be done onshore, offshore and in Alaska.

The economy needs to offset the need for imported oil in every manner possible and the country needs the income. Technology has evolved to the point where these reserves can be responsibly developed in an environmentally safe manner.

Technology has also greatly improved the cleanliness of burning coal. Coal resource development needs to be expanded and clean coal burning plants built. There are vast reserves of undeveloped coal and it makes no sense not to utilize the resource. All coal on federal lands should be used to strengthen the economy and reduce the dependence on foreign energy sources.

There is a potential for an expansion of hydroelectric power in the country. Any existing facilities need to be upgraded and expanded. More generators should be built at existing plants wherever possible. Dams need to be managed to keep them as full as possible at all times to ensure a safe and consistent power supply. It makes no sense to spill water into the ocean without generating as much power as possible on the way.

These are all true stimulus initiatives that will generate revenues for the government and reduce taxes to the people.

"Behind the ostensible government sits enthroned an invisible government owing no allegiance and acknowledging no responsibility to the people."

Theodore Roosevelt

Chapter 18

Corporate Bailouts

Our economic system is designed to allow successfully managed businesses to prosper and the inefficient and weak to fail and fall away. It has been that way since before the founding of the country and it must be that way now. Bailouts don't work and never will.

It is said that Chrysler was bailed out years ago and it worked then, why won't it work now? Well, the fact is Chrysler was "loaned out", not bailed out. Chrysler paid the government back hundreds of millions of dollars and labor unions made huge concessions or that program would not have worked.

Iacocca and team also redesigned the entire fleet to create a product that would sell at a profit. Add to that the fact that the restrictions placed on the auto companies back then were nothing like they are today. It is not a fair comparison between then and now.

Get real about what has happened and will continue to happen in the 2009 situation. Those companies that have received bailout funds are coming back for more. They will keep coming back and coming back. They are unsuccessfully operated companies and have been living on poor management, greed and speculation for years. Government can't save them.

It would take reconstructing these companies from the ground up to save them and that isn't going to happen if they are bailed out. They continue to be managed by the same policies and boards of directors as they were before, so there is just more and more of the same. Labor unions have conceded little or nothing.

The only thing that will save these bailout companies, whether they are insurance companies, banks or auto companies is to let them fail. Put them into bankruptcy and sell them off piece by piece and jobs will be absorbed into the takeover companies and preserved.

To let them continue to operate in their inefficient ways will lead to shut down companies and lost jobs, many of these jobs permanently lost. It is shear lunacy to pour taxpayer money into these loser companies. These losers will eventually be in bankruptcy anyway and all the bailout money will then be completely lost.

The same applies to the mortgage bailout. 90% plus of American homeowners are going to bailout less than 10% of the inefficient losers of the housing market. It is insanity for the successful to bailout the unsuccessful. Wake up America!

It is impossible to spend anything rich. That has never worked in the history of the world. This bailout business is what happens when we have a government run by entrenched, career politicians with no business experience.

Why would America expect that any of these politicians would be able to run any business? If there were business people in the congress we would not be in this mess. That is why the stock market may drop to 3000 or below.

Business and investors know government cannot run a business and entrenched politicians are not businessmen. This is the Stimulus Tragedy.

"We are not afraid to entrust the American people with unpleasant facts, foreign ideas, alien philosophies, and competitive values. For a nation that is afraid to let its people judge the truth and falsehood in an open market is a nation that is afraid of its people."

John F. Kennedy

Chapter 19

Free Trade

Free trade is one of the most discriminatory practices in place in the world today. Initiated by the United States in the form of policy for decades and by law for the past 20 or so years, it is one of the worst things to have happened in America. It is discriminatory against the people it was supposed to help – **WE THE PEOPLE**.

Free trade, as we know it in America, helps our trading partners at the expense of United States business and workers. No other country in the world allows imported goods to displace the jobs of their people.

There is no free trade for America. Our jobs and exports are denied by countries all over the world and used as State Department pawns in negotiations with other countries under the guise of free trade. Yet another example of entrenched, career politicians pretending to be businessmen. These free trade policies must stop.

Fair trade is to be the new terminology. Fair trade means any country importing goods to America takes goods back. Cars for wheat. Shirts for beef. Televisions for tractors. IPods for timber. No fair trade – no imports.

This is not to be confused with establishing trade barriers with other countries, but rather a dollar for dollar barter type exchange. Importers take the equivalent of exchange goods until Americas export goods are transferred. It is a simple and efficient fair trade policy.

With fair trade policies replacing free trade policies, markets in many commodities and goods will be stabilized.

Imagine a sensible policy of grain exports in a dollar for dollar barter type exchange. There would be no need for farm subsidies saving billions in tax dollars. Farmers will make money and in turn purchase new farm machinery and on and on it goes.

This is true stimulus.

"It may be laid down as a primary position, and the basis of our system, that every citizen who enjoys the protection of free government, owes not only a proportion of his property, but even his personal services to the defense of it."

George Washington

Chapter 20

Defense and Military

No matter how bad the economy gets America must have a strong military. In fact, the worse the economy gets the more important it is to have a strong military.

The entrenched are cutting the military at a time of greatest need. Never will America be as vulnerable as during a recession. Never do the entrenched try harder to cut the military than during a recession. It is always the case and always will be. Yet another case why politicians are not successful in business. Nothing they do makes any sense.

The defense of **WE THE PEOPLE** is a first priority. In order to keep the people safe it is imperative that the military be strong. No greater deterrent to terrorism exists than a strong military. The military must be continually refreshed and upgraded to keep our country safe.

Cutting the military sends the message to any potential enemies that America is soft and weak. Our great country must never find itself in a pre World War II position of weakness.

With the continuing military operations in Iraq and Afghanistan every effort must be made to support that effort with adequate measures to complete the job and supply the troops. Any cuts in military budgets will add to troop casualties and lengthen the mission. This must not be allowed to happen. All Americans owe their freedom to the efforts of a strong military and that will be the case in the future as well.

The Mexican situation will spill into the United States some time very soon. It may be necessary to expend troops to maintain the safety of America. At such a time as the Mexican government loses the ability to slow this situation it will roar into the United States and our military may be required to stop it.

Since the entrenched don't have the common sense, the will or the guts to address this situation in a responsible way, it will likely end up that the military will be battling these drug runners in the streets of America.

The longer that border remains unsecured the more likely this will happen in a large way. It is happening now, but not in a big enough way to get action from the entrenched.

There are other reasons to be concerned with a weak military. Iran and Korea are two.

At this point in time, a strong military and support of it is true stimulus.

"Allow the president to invade a neighboring nation, whenever he shall deem it necessary to repel an invasion, and you allow him to do so whenever he may choose to say he deems it necessary for such a purpose; and you allow him to make war at pleasure."

Abraham Lincoln

Chapter 21

War

There is nothing to be gained in this book by offering opinions regarding whether or not America needed to become involved in any current or previous military action. Most sensible people do not like war.

We have lost far too many young men and women in military actions in the history of this nation. That is a very sad thing.

Since World War II, America has taken it upon itself to be the world police. It is very disconcerting that our country continues to enter into police actions around the world. To think we need to be a military presence all around the world is very disturbing and much of the world hates us for it.

It doesn't make sense for America to put our military in peril and spend needed taxpayer money to support it. We simply can't afford to police the world. America must utilize the military to defend the country, not police the world. For this country to remain great these police actions must be limited.

When these actions are necessary to protect **WE THE PEOPLE**, then we need to allow the military to do their job and then get out as quickly as possible.

The entrenched start wars and then demand the military to clean up their messes. For decades these actions have been made into political wars. They are started, funded and controlled by entrenched, career politicians. This must stop!

Also, it is total insanity for the military to put up with the intrusion of the press when trying to do their job. The time has long since come when press reporting is done by a military press corps. It costs lives to fight wars with the unlimited press coverage as it exists today.

With regard to terrorism, there is only one efficient way for the military to remove the threat. It is a much simpler and cost effective method than full scale war. Your military is well suited to do it and they know how to do it.

At such time as the victims of terrorism, that is **WE THE PEOPLE**, go after specific individual terrorists, it will be very difficult to stop them. The other side of that nickel is at such time that the specific, individual terrorists know they are the end target, will this situation begin to be controlled.

These fanatics need to know their lives are at great risk and they will be vigorously pursued until eliminated and they will not be martyred.

Whatever measures are necessary to locate the leaders of terrorism and eliminate them must be a top priority. No pictures of dead bodies or any press releases, they just disappear, permanently.

This does not involve large numbers of troops and maybe no troops at all. It may need to be done through the underground using innovative means. If the military is used it will be done by highly trained special forces to pursue and destroy.

More resources must be devoted to intelligence. The government needs to know precisely what action is required and be able to verify this information to **WE THE PEOPLE**. Never again must there be questions regarding intelligence like what took place after the Iraq invasion.

Unfortunately, the CIA is under constant attack from the entrenched, which makes intelligence gathering a marginalized effort. The biggest reason for this is the entrenched don't have enough control over the CIA and they hate anything they can't totally control. In order to keep American safe, intelligence efforts must be expanded, not curtailed.

These terrorist fanatics are not going to go away. The reality is that the Mexican drug gang situation has created a whole new category of terrorist. They are all terrorists, just the same, and must be destroyed.

Terrorists understand only attack and thereby they must be defeated in the same way. This must be done behind the scenes and out of the news.

What terrorists understand is terror and they must be made to feel the same terror as that felt by their victims. They need to know they are marked and acts of terrorism will not be tolerated by America.

Again, this is not about whether or not America needed to be in any previous war. What it is about is keeping **WE THE PEOPLE** safe and how to keep the costs of doing so as low as possible.

"Oil is like a wild animal. Whoever captures it has it."

J. Paul Getty

Chapter 22

The Oil Opportunity

The oil crisis is not a crisis. It is an opportunity. An opportunity for technology and innovation to rise to a new level. Already the technology exists to replace oil. If allowed to, the entrepreneurial spirit of America will remove the dependence on oil worldwide.

With regard to oil the biggest challenge to achieving independence is government policy. As always, the entrenched are in the way. Idiotic tax policy, government regulation and endless bureaucracy are hindering the entrepreneurial spirit.

Government, for all it tells us, is firmly in the way. Until the entrenched, career politician is removed from office and all the special interest favors are gone with them, the goal of oil independence cannot be achieved.

Special effort needs to be made to replace oil in motor vehicles. The technology is already there to do it. Of course, there are issues to be worked out, but the technology is already here.

Given free rein, the spirit of man will solve any technological issues very quickly. However, giving up control of the process is not in the best interest of the entrenched. There are too many regulations and government agencies involved in this process.

If the entrenched will stay out of the way, new technologies will appear that will dramatically improve the efficiency of the internal combustion engine.

As a result the supplies of oil will be stretched by many years beyond what the projections are today. In short, the oil crisis is going to be minimized and by the time the supplies are gone, if that ever happens, it will not be an issue.

What needs to be done today is for the government to fill to capacity all oil storage available in the strategic oil reserves and keep them full. These supplies will save the day in the event that any sort of situation arises that prevents accessing imported oil.

It must also be a priority to develop all available domestic oil resources in a sensible, environmentally responsible way. The technology already exists, but only if the entrenched get out of the way. Once these measures are taken, America's dependence on imported oil is dramatically reduced.

Then make it a priority to enter into trade agreements for the importation of oil and natural gas from Mexico and Canada. Expansion of oil production in Mexico will be a life changing economic event for them.

All oil coming from Mexico will be used to keep the strategic reserves at capacity first, because of the accessibility issues, and then sell the balance.

Both Canada and Mexico are going to need this trade to provide stability to their economies. This is a positive long term benefit to both Mexico and Canada.

By this time America's dependence on imported oil will have been mostly eliminated. Then apply a per barrel import tax on all oil imported from any other source. This revenue will be used exclusively for the development of alternative sources of energy to replace oil.

This will require diligent monitoring by **WE THE PEOPLE** as the entrenched will try to side track it to other pet projects. Energy costs worldwide will once again be based on a supply and demand market which will be a cost saving to the entire world.

The power of OPEC to dictate the price of oil will be eliminated. They will continue to have huge revenues, but their revenues will be based on fair market prices.

If oil dependence is a major issue within the next 20 years, it will be because **WE THE PEOPLE** became complacent and allowed the current entrenched to remain in office or allowed another generation of entrenched to become established.

Also of benefit to these changes is the issue of the questionable science of global warming, which will go away with it, at least as far as America is concerned.

"Water is the driving force of all nature."

Leonardo da Vinci

Chapter 23

Water

Over the next 100 years water, not oil and not global warming will be the crisis. But, only if plans are not made now to prevent it.

America uses a lot of water. Population will continue to grow, and as the entrenched are removed from office the economy will blossom. The result will be an increase in the use of water. Plans must be implemented now to expand and conserve water.

It is difficult to envision the United States in a water crisis. The country is blessed with seemingly abundant water resources. But if we look closely there are water shortages in large areas of the country now.

The Great Plains states and high plains states are largely dry areas. Ground water has been short in Eastern Colorado, Kansas, Oklahoma and Western Texas forever. Large areas of New Mexico, Utah, Arizona and California are desert or dry lands.

For the United States to be strong and safe, it needs to be able to sustain itself. For that to continue into the next century, plans must be made to ensure an adequate supply of water for agriculture. This water must be clean and environmentally safe.

There must be reserves that can be called upon in times of drought to sustain agriculture. The country must have the means to transport water to areas of drought to ensure a consistent food supply.

Presently there are millions of acres of tillable land that produce little or nothing because there is no way to get water to them. A plan to conserve, move and store water needs to be implemented. All care must be taken to store water in existing reservoirs and keep these as close to full as possible at all times. Canals and pipelines need to be built to move water to farm lands and cities.

In exchange for the allowing the importation of oil and natural gas from Canada to the United States, without the imported oil tax as mentioned in the oil chapter, a water use and transportation agreement must be made with Canada.

Canada is water rich. The United States needs to trade with Canada for water that can be brought by canal into the Missouri River system in Montana. From there it can be transported by canal and/or pipeline to all areas east of the Rocky Mountains. The same needs to be done west of the Rocky Mountains.

If there is not enough water in the Columbia Basin to supply the Colorado River system, then Canadian trade agreements must be established.

At some point it will become necessary to decide if water is going to be provided to Las Vegas and fancy golf courses in the southwest or if there will be food on the table.

Already California has water shortages that adversely affect agriculture and the cities. Southern California uses a lot of water and needs much more.

The Colorado River delta in Mexico has been mostly dry for many years as the water is used up before it gets there. Many millions of acres of prime delta farm land lie unproductive as a result and it has negatively changed the lives of hundreds of thousands of Mexicans.

This is an issue that will never be admitted to or addressed by the entrenched. Only by replacing them with fresh, open minded idea people will this situation be addressed. That is until it does become a crisis, which it will. The time to begin studying and planning is now.

"An enemy generally says and believes what he wishes."

Thomas Jefferson

Chapter 24

Trading with the Enemy

For decades the United States has been sending huge sums of cash to countries that are a threat to **WE THE PEOPLE**. Others are openly unfriendly. This is a policy that must be stopped.

John McCain stated in the 2008 campaign that $75 billion is being sent to these countries. That is a lot of cash that comes out of the pockets of taxpayers. It is a small amount compared to the trillions of dollars that are going to be committed by the entrenched over the next few years, but it would be a pretty fair balance in your checkbook.

The entrenched maintain that most of this money is going for human rights issues and that to remove it would cause famine and disease to claim millions of people.

The opponents of this spending claim that this money is going to dictators and despots and ends up supporting a lavish lifestyle for the elite and much of it ends up in the hands of terrorists.

The question has to be whether or not this money is better spent at home during a difficult economic time or given away to foreigners.

There are many countries that receive aid from America. There are many starving, diseased people in the world. No one denies these things.

The critical issue with this argument is how to get aid to the people and not into the hands of dictators, despots and terrorists. Any spending that does not go directly into the hands of the needy must stop.

Spending going to countries that are openly unfriendly or are determined to hurt Americans must be stopped. Once that decision is made it can then be determined how to help people in those countries that need food and medical assistance. America is a generous country.

American's are willing to give. If not they wouldn't allow spending for foreign aid in the first place. The trick is to even know if, or how much our government is giving and how it is being used.

The solution to foreign spending is to be sure any monies spent for food and medical assistance are distributed directly to those in need by private entities with a proven track record of getting the product to the right people. That way it serves a good purpose and actually helps people in need. This method of distribution is common sense and moral.

Going back to the first paragraph, money going directly to foreign governments unfriendly or hostile to **WE THE PEOPLE**, must stop. $75 billion is a huge amount of money you need to keep at home.

This is true stimulus.

"The sum of wisdom is that time is never lost that is devoted to work."

Ralph Waldo Emerson

Chapter 25

Labor Unions and Card Check

This is going to be a short chapter. The reason for that is that labor unions are good and harmful at the same time. Employers are the same way. There are two sides to the argument and they both have valid points.

Card Check is a plan devised by labor unions with the goal in mind to force union membership on all business. If you are employed by a non union business you must think this through. Your job may well depend on whether or not you allow the federal government to implement Card Check.

Upon passage, you can be required, under law, to pay union dues. Passage of Card Check imposes, under law, another tax on the worker. Card Check will force businesses to close all across the nation.

Most small businesses cannot afford to be unionized, from a dollar and cents standpoint. Card Check is an assault on your individual freedom pure and simple.

Here is the whole thing. The right to work is not a federal issue. It is a state issue. To have the entrenched in federal government dictating to the states regarding this issue is not in the best interest of the worker.

Every state has different types of businesses and geographical issues. It is impossible to create a federal law that is applicable and workable in every state. Card Check on the federal level is a poor idea.

Wages and types of jobs vary greatly from state to state. It would be a discriminatory practice and is likely unconstitutional. Many small businesses could not afford it and jobs would be lost.

This is not a good idea for troubled times. Or for the workers or the states.

"Socialism is a philosophy of failure, the creed of ignorance, and the gospel of envy, its inherent virtue is the sharing of misery."

Winston Churchill

Chapter 26

Socialized Medicine

If enacted, Socialized medicine will be the most expensive progressive and permanent spending program in the history of the nation. It will make Social Security, Medicare and Medicaid look like an evening at the movies, by comparison.

Think about it this way. You are about to see Social Security go away because it will not support itself and that is with the entire nation making payments into it since 1935. Whenever you get a paycheck there is a deduction on your check marked FICA.

The 2008 rate for this non tax deductable item is 6.2% of your income up $106,800 and then there is additional deduction for Medicare of 1.45% with no earning limit. Added to that, your employer is forced to pay the same 6.2% and 1.45% to your credit, for a total of 15.3%. Self employed people pay the entire 15.3% and that includes most small business owners.

Social Security is broke and a part of the stimulus bill goes to states to shore up Medicaid which is also broke.

So, the entrenched are taking 15.3% of your hard earned money for Social Security and Medicaid now. Can you afford socialized medicine? Are you willing to pay another 15-20% of your salary for it?

Here are the realities of how the entrenched manage your affairs in Washington, DC. You are paying 15.3% of your income to Social Security now. They are determined to, and will pass, a socialized medicine bill, **if you let them**.

It is going to cost you somewhere between 15 and 30% of your income in some way in the form of taxes.

Add to that income taxes of:
- 10% if you earn under $8,025
- 15% if you earn $8,025 - $32,500
- 25% if you earn $32,500 - $78,850
- 28% if you earn $78,850 - $164,550
- 33% if you earn $164,550 - $357,700
- 35% if you earn $357,500 and above
- most of these rates are going up.

Are you willing to pay 30% to 60% in taxes to the entrenched so they can break the programs and waste your money as in bailouts and all sorts of other insane ways? And do it this year and next year in the midst of the worst economic downturn since the early 1980's?

Add to this all sorts of back door taxes that will likely raise these rates another 10 or more percent. Think about it. These entrenched, career politicians are going to set you up to pay rates like this for the rest of your life, **if you let them**.

Remember, the entrenched don't have to pay their taxes and they get big retirement checks and paid medical for life, and, and, and _ _ _. Top that off with the tax collector; Treasury Secretary, Tim Geitner, a tax cheat and manager of the IRS, who announced recently that the IRS was going to go after those of you not paying your taxes.

Remember what was said in earlier chapters regarding the tactics of the IRS?

The hypocrisy of the entrenched knows no bounds.

The solution to Socialized Medicine is to be found in the chapter "The Tax Solution". The worker, the family and small businesses need a break.

When the proposals adopted in that previous chapter are adopted, the aforementioned will be able to purchase medical insurance.

Additionally, forcing people earning under $32,500 to pay 10% - 15% or more in tax is unconscionable, in the first place.

It is no wonder so many people are hurting. It's all about spending. If the entrenched don't spend, you don't pay.

It is totally up to us, **WE THE PEOPLE,** how far we let this go. At some point it will may irreversible. Say no to Socialized Medicine.

"Knowledge will forever govern ignorance; and a people who mean to be their own governors must arm themselves with the power which knowledge gives."

James Madison

Chapter 27

Education

WE THE PEOPLE must take control of America's education system. The future of this great land depends on our young people. These young people must have access to and receive a top quality education. This is not happening.

Education must include the basic skills required to have a working knowledge of those things that make a real difference in day-to-day life.

Specialized studies are fine, but only after reaching a point of practical learning with regard to a basic, working knowledge of day-to-day life skills. Young people need to know how to read, write, add and subtract. This is not happening in education today.

To prove this, ask any store clerk to count your change back to you. Ask someone to read something out loud. Many people cannot read or even have a basic understanding of the English language. It is appalling!

Once the foundation of basic knowledge is in place, it is then a logical, common sense move into basic bookkeeping, computers and whatever additional skills are required to function in the world today.

There is no limit to what can be taught in the schools. Whatever skills are required at any point in time can be easily adapted into a system that teaches basic and specific knowledge.

Without the basics the system continues to turn out illiterates who are totally unable to function in the world, at any level.

Upon learning to read and write, a student can then be taught an understanding of history. America is crumbling due to the lack of teaching the fundamentals of government. This refers to the fundamentals of American government and the history thereof.

American education has become biased against the fundamental principles of the founders of this country. If America is going to continue to be the greatest nation in the history of the world; young Americans must learn the basic fundamental principles this country was founded upon.

The educational system must put the good of the individual first and educate them as to what risks and sacrifices were made by the founders upon the writing of the Declaration of Independence and the subsequent signing of that document.

Education must teach the young the Constitution and Bill of Rights and show them how to apply these majestic documents in day-to-day life. This is not being done today.

Basic education involves a working knowledge of reading, writing and practical math. Those skills are further developed with a detailed and unbiased study of government at the root level.

That is at the level of the Declaration of Independence, the Constitution and Bill of Rights. Only upon building a strong base of knowledge involving these basic studies will the young people be assured of maintaining the life of freedom and unlimited opportunities America presently offers to all citizens.

Establishing education at this level is of primary importance to the survival of America as we now know it.

Educators are key in this process. There are estimated to be 3.5 million educators in America.

That sounds like a lot of people, but it is a minute percentage compared to the 300 million or more people in the country requiring education.

It is important that educators are well paid to attract the best people to the profession. It is equally important that educators be held responsible for the way they teach.

Most people remember some excellent teachers in their educational lives. Most also remember some very bad ones, as well.

WE THE PEOPLE have a right to expect the best from educators and in turn for that fair pay and benefits. The curriculum is the responsibility of all involved in the process and must have at the base the founding American documents and principles.

The most important thing in education is the student. Young people are the future of America and the world. All young people must know they can be all they make up their minds to be and be taught that from the very first day of schooling.

They need to know there is no limit to the opportunity for any person in America who will study, dream, set goals and work hard. Students must be infused with enthusiasm for freedom, education and opportunity.

It is the responsibility of every parent, teacher, administrator and government official to be a moral and principled example and inspiration to the young.

A government of **WE THE PEOPLE** will maintain itself and prosper only when disciplined.

"With malice toward none, with charity for all,, with firmness in the right, as God gives us to see the right, let us strive on to finish the work we are in, to bind up the nation's wounds."

Abraham Lincoln

Chapter 28

Mid Term Elections

WE THE PEOPLE have an opportunity to begin a process of correction in the mid-term elections of 2010. Information is available online to study the arguments regarding this proposal. Aggressive, positive and immediate action is required!

These elections may be the most important mid terms in the history of America. Every American must wake up to what is happening in our great country and make every effort to remove the entrenched, career politicians from government.

Now is the time to be selecting qualified candidates to run opposite every entrenched, career politician up for reelection. It is important to begin this process now. Finding qualified candidates who are willing to run is not an easy task.

Most of the best people are busy trying to survive this economic wreck. The best qualified candidates are likely to be small business people and they are getting hammered in this economy and will be reluctant to leave their businesses.

For an aspiring politician the move to Washington is a dream to be realized. For a small business person it is a totally different thing. They have to sacrifice family, business, a good life and expose themselves to the public spotlight and the scrutiny of a merciless press.

It is something most of the best people are unwilling to do. It is up to us to find those who will and encourage and support them.

There are questions that must be asked of our candidates. It is very important to get an affirmative answer to questions relating to the Constitution. It is imperative the candidate have an unwavering set of principles where Constitutional issues are concerned.

To be effective the candidate must be willing to stand firm on Constitutional principles regardless of party affiliation.

We need to have full confidence the candidate is putting the Constitution first in the best interest of **WE THE PEOPLE**. If there is any doubt about this we have not found the candidate needed to reverse the current situation.

The reason for this is the entrenched may be slowed down if our candidate wins election, but those who are left are going to be running scared and will resort to any measures to further their agenda. This will be particularly true if our candidate is a Democrat.

It is going to take a lot of courage and principle for our candidate to withstand this assault. Should our newly elected candidate be weak, they will be marginalized and consumed.

Remember what has happened and what is continuing to happen with regard to attacks on the Constitution and runaway government spending.

It will be necessary to monitor and support our candidate to keep them focused on the mission at hand. Everything discussed so far in this book hinges on these mid-term elections.

Should the entrenched not be weakened in these mid-term elections and the blind euphoria of the 2008 elections carry through to the 2012 elections and the entrenched remain in power, whatever has happened up to that point will pale in comparison to what the years 2012 to 2016 will bring!

Our future is in our hands. It is up to us.

"Important principles may, and must, be inflexible."

Abraham Lincoln

Chapter 29

The New President

For America to survive, recover and maintain our lives as they have been it is critical that a new President be elected in 2012. There are no words to adequately express how important this is to the country.

This is not a normal election or a normal time. The current President and his agenda will destroy American life as it exists today. This is not an overstatement but rather an understatement.

The rate of the growth of government that will be seen between 2009 and the end of 2012 will stagger the imagination. It is impossible to picture what will happen during those years. If the wheels stop turning in the current direction in early 2009 it will still be the largest growth of government and debt in American history.

These things may be unsustainable in the best of times and the country is not in the best of times.

The mid-term elections of 2010 will likely be the most important in American history, but the Presidential election of 2012 will likely be the most important of any time.

It is important to keep in mind, no matter how serious the current situation is, it can be reversed, if **WE THE PEOPLE** take immediate, positive and aggressive action. America must keep the faith and tackle this situation with all the will it possesses. Here is the way to do it.

As mentioned earlier in this book, both the Republican and Democratic parties are badly broken. The Democrats have been gloating over the fact that they won everything in the 2008 elections. The

Republicans are hanging their heads in defeat and blaming each other for their failures. It is a truly sorry mess and America is suffering for it.

The entrenched from both parties are so wrapped up in partisan politics they can't see the sun. How long are **WE THE PEOPLE** going to tolerate this? Hopefully, the end of the nonsense is at hand.

In the 1990's we saw a similar situation only it was the Republicans who won control of Congress. We will never forget the arrogance of the victors as they marched into the grand halls of our Congress to take the oath of office. And, **WE THE PEOPLE** took action and within two years that situation had begun to change.

The difference between then and now is that in the 1990's we had a Democratic President. There was some separation of power. The present situation is all loaded one way and the entrenched are having a grand time, at our expense.

The separation of power as provided by the Constitution was a result of contentious debate by the founders. The Constitution came about after endless sessions over a considerable time. It took much compromise to come up with a finished document.

Without this contentious debate our Constitution would have been loaded to one side or the other and likely would have been ineffective or an outright failure.

What did happen was that the most unusual and effective government the world has ever seen was the result. Our government is designed to be contentious. By design it works the best when there are differing views and sensible debate.

The process is set up in the Constitution to be this way because it was written in the spirit of compromise. Had the founders not compromised the Constitution would not exist as we know it.

The entrenched have circumvented due process under the premise of emergency with the stimulus bill. They are daily circumventing the process with every piece of legislation that has hit the floor since the 2008 election.

For the next two years there is no way to stop this. The minority does not have the power to force due process or force any sort of compromise. The entire legislative process is now broken as a result.

At no time since the founding of America has the legislative process been subverted like this. **WE THE PEOPLE** are about to lose the foundation of our country.

We must elect a new President in the 2012 election to save the country as we now know it.

This candidate is going to have to run as a Republican to do it. If that doesn't put a hopeless feeling in our hearts, nothing will.

The Republicans are beyond broken, they are smashed. No one is in sight to lead them. There is no Ronald Reagan on the horizon. Too bad, the country needs one right now. All we see are the losers of the last election.

Any candidates in sight are worn out. That does not mean they are not good people. Some of them are great Americans, patriots and very good, principled people. But, they are political rejects. They were defeated in primaries and general elections.

They are forgotten names in a party of no names. It has gotten so bad that recently a radio talk show commentator was purported to be the leader of the party. What a sad state of affairs for **WE THE PEOPLE**.

So, what are we to do? Our candidate must run as a Republican. An independent candidate would faction the votes needed to remove the current President. The only chance we have is to leave Washington and find an ordinary citizen to be the candidate.

It is difficult to find a candidate for Congress and this one is much more critical than a candidate for the mid terms. But there is good news. That person does exist, somewhere.

The biggest challenge we have is that partisan politics factors into this search. The Republicans will be looking at Republican governors and entrenched Senators. That is where they always look.

The person who will be able to carry this off is an ordinary man or woman hidden in a small business somewhere and may not even be in the Republican Party. If the Republicans are unable to open their minds and find someone like this, they will fail.

What does this person look like? Who is this person? First, the new President must have the principles of the Constitution as a firmly grounded ideal.

Secondly, these principles must be, as written, intended and clearly stated in the Constitution, in the best interest of **WE THE PEOPLE**.

Those are the two most important ideals. In fact, they are the only ideals that can reverse the present direction of government. Add to those the courage, strength and presence to hold to those ideals at all times, in every decision.

The new President must have the principles of a Ronald Reagan and the guts of a Harry Truman. This person must be able to rise above partisan politics at all times and always put the principles and interests of the Constitution and **WE THE PEOLPLE** above all else.

This must not be about political parties but about what is best for the country. The Republican Party must put all partisan ideologies aside. If the Republicans can do this and follow the other ideas set forth in this chapter, they will succeed and it will be in the best interests of America and **WE THE PEOPLE**.

It remains to be seen if they have the courage, common sense and will to do this. If not it will be the end of the Republican Party and a new conservative party will become the dominant second party.

While this is happening the government will continue to grow, spending will continue unchecked, taxes will continue to rise and life as we know it will be changed forever.

We will begin to live like Cubans.

Since the Republican Party is essentially smashed at this time it will take an unprecedented series of events for them to pull this off. There will have to be a revolution fully in motion by the time of the Republican convention in 2012.

It will not be the Republican Party allowing this to take place. **WE THE PEOPLE** will have to force the Republican Party to do the right thing. The voters of America will have to be marching in the streets with such a strong voice the Republicans will be forced to submit to our wishes.

During the race for the candidacy of the Republican nomination, it must appear all is running the same as it always has. Primary elections roll along as they always have and the voters continue to play the game as always.

The Republican Party will have a group of the same old faces and names running and the voters will be uncooperative because they will know the person they need is not coming from within these ranks.

The revolution will pick up momentum and the Republicans will appear to be unresponsive. Then at the Republican convention, the party must unveil their candidate with no previous knowledge of this person to the delegates or the public.

The new President will appear on stage and announce to the country that they are the candidate and will represent the Republicans in the 2012 election. Only this method will excite the voters and generate the support necessary to get their candidate elected. The excitement must be genuine and overwhelming.

Desperate times call for desperate measures. The Republicans must win the 2012 election. There is no other way to reverse the current direction of government.

The current President will run as an incumbent so the reversal must come from the Republicans. There is no other way. So, the Republicans, at the highest level, must begin now to find and select the person who will be charged with saving the country.

This must be done quietly and without dissent. The factions of the Republican Party now fighting amongst themselves must unite and do the right thing.

They must be disciplined enough to find a commoner to run for this office, totally outside of any currently existing selection processes.

There are millions of Americans more aptly qualified and competent to serve as President than the current President.

It is imperative the Republicans find one of these people, convince them to run and keep their identity completely secret until they walk onto the stage at the convention.

Finding a qualified and competent candidate is the easy part of this. Convincing the candidate to put everything they have worked for on the line and exposing themselves, their families and their businesses to all the downsides of running for the office is the hard part.

It is always the biggest challenge of the Republican Party to select willing candidates. Most people who would make the best candidates are not willing to run. They must give up too much; it is not worth the sacrifices involved.

It is the job of the Republican Party to think outside the box and find this person at all costs. **WE THE PEOPLE** demand it!

The young of America are the victims of present policy; and at the same time, the future and the hope. For this plan to be successful, the candidate must appeal to the young voter. Ideally, the candidate will be in the range of 45 – 55 years of age.

If someone with all the attributes of Reagan were to be the candidate the age will not make a difference. They must have the charisma of an Obama, a Clinton or a Reagan.

The candidate must be prepared to express their ideals to the young of America in writing prior to the election.

Young people are perceptive and intelligent. They will not elect a Republican candidate on the basis of change, not knowing what that change is to be. One time with that has been enough. Only with the support of the young voter will the new President be elected.

Getting the intellectuals and the entrenched in the Republican Party to entertain such an idea is going to be interesting to watch. Frankly, it is more likely they will continue to bicker and banter and slide into oblivion.

Hopefully, that won't happen. If **WE THE PEOPLE** rise up in revolution, in enough numbers, expressing dissatisfaction and intolerance of things as they are, the Republican Party may come around.

That is the hope.

For America to reverse the current direction and become a nation of responsible government, of and for the people, there must be a qualified and competent Republican candidate in the White House in January 2013.

"The seed of revolution is repression."

Woodrow Wilson

Chapter 30

Revolution

What form of revolution do you prefer? A civil war like the last one? A taxpayer revolt? A voter revolt?

America is heading for a revolution. It is inevitable. The entrenched are pushing us into to it. The entrenched start wars and revolts as a matter of practice and they do it in the same ways all over the world.

The manifestations may differ, but the cause remains the same. Revolution is always a result of the few pushing their ideologies and policies on the many. History is loaded with the same stories played out in differing degrees all over the world. It is time for **WE THE PEOPLE** to revolt!

Of course, no one would ever want to see a civil war like the last one. A taxpayer revolt may be necessary if a voter revolt is unsuccessful.

It is much easier to initiate revolution in the form of a voter revolt than either of the other two choices. At this point in time a voter revolt is the only viable option.

Tax revolt will happen at such time as we just can't survive and pay the tax, but by then we will be living on the streets. Old fashioned civil war then becomes necessary to remain alive and the result is a civil war like the French Revolution.

The entrenched must be made to know and understand a revolution is being formed and will precipitate aggressive, positive and immediate action.

All common sense Americans must rise up and be heard. At the time of this writing the entrenched have not heard us. They continue, unfettered, to spend us into oblivion and destroy our rights.

Only **WE THE PEOPLE** can stop it. The many must rise up against the few, and DO IT NOW!

WE THE PEOPLE have the right to stand up against tyranny and defend the Constitution from without or from within. America is now experiencing tyranny from within.

What is happening in America is tyranny, pure and simple; perpetrated by entrenched, career politicians in the federal government.

The entrenched are destroying our country, our way of life and those of our children and descendents for generations yet unborn and maybe forever.

It is a classic case of the few destroying the lives of the many. Unfortunately, most Americans haven't figured it out, yet. Over time most of them will, but America doesn't have any time.

The wheels are firmly in motion and unless aggressive, positive and immediate action is taken very soon, it may be too late. The revolution must begin now and with enough force to create fear in the hearts of every one of the entrenched.

These entrenched are unconscious and America can only get their attention by taking aggressive, positive and immediate action. Only when injected with fear for the loss of their power and control over **WE THE PEOPLE** will they hear us and listen to us. The individual must exercise their full power to save America's way of life.

Waiting to see what happens is suicidal. Most Americans are hoping the entrenched will come to their senses. Everyday America is told spending our money for multiple generations is good for us.

The tendency is to "just give it a chance" and that is what the entrenched are telling us over and over every day. Every day they spend hundreds of billions more. It is a never ending river of ever larger spending.

Begin the revolution, NOW! Call, write, email or fax your congressional delegation and tell them you will not tolerate them destroying our lives and those of our families. Do it every day. Take a few minutes and do it.

Begin now to focus on the mid-term elections of 2010 and find quality candidates to run for office with the goal in mind of unseating every one of the entrenched who voted for any of this insane spending.

Tell them now is not the time to obligate us to trillions of dollars in costs for Socialized Medicine. Tell them to initiate the tax cuts explained in the chapter "The Tax Solution".

Tell them we will tolerate no more spending. Become active in getting the 49,000,000 eligible voters registered who did not vote in the 2008 elections.

Search for qualified and competent people to run as the Republican candidate for President in the 2012 election and let the Republicans in your area know who these people are.

Wake up America! Revolt, and DO IT NOW! Our way of life depends on it.

"Let us not seek the Republican answer or the Democratic answer, but the right answer. Let us not seek to fix the blame for the past. Let us accept our own responsibility for the future."

John F. Kennedy

Chapter 31

The Future

The United States of America will persevere. In what form remains to be seen. The direction of government since the 2008 elections is away from fiscal responsibility and individual rights and towards endless debt, a reduced standard of living and less individual freedom.

Runaway spending by itself is enough to permanently degrade the American standard of living and way of life.

Spending requires more taxes to fund it and that relates to less money in the hands of the taxpayer, which is you. New government programs cost us even more.

More power is destined to be in hands of the few and that minimizes the many, which is you. **WE THE PEOPLE** are well on the way to becoming indentured servants to the entrenched.

Our lifestyle is rapidly being compromised. America is looking more like Cuba everyday.

Take a few minutes and inventory in your mind, or on paper, what you have today. Examine your incomes, your take home pay, your bank balances, what your insurances cost, what your wardrobe looks like, what your cars look like, what your leisure activities look like and keep that inventory in mind or at hand.

Write down the interest rates on your home and your cars. Inventory your family and friends. Note how they are living, what they own and where they work. Go online and research inflation rates.

Note the names of your Representatives and Senators and keep notes on their voting records. Do this so you can refer back to it over the next few years and see what your life looks like then compared to now.

What any American has, how they live and where they work depends entirely on what course **WE THE PEOPLE** allow the government to take from this day forward. The future holds many variables.

What is certain is common sense and history both say that unless aggressive, positive and immediate action is taken NOW, every American, other than the entrenched, will have less. It can be no other way.

Even if you are a stanch Obama supporter and/or Democrat, common sense is telling you these policies can't work.

The little voice in the back of your mind is telling you that you can't spend yourself rich and if you manage your own life the way the entrenched are managing your government you will be broke and will eventually be living on the street.

You know, really, what is happening is not going to work. You are hoping in some way there will be some stimulated money coming back to you and you can survive.

You are beginning to get small subconscious messages that whatever problems the country had prior to the elections of 2008 are worsening and, in fact, you were better off at that time than you are now.

It is becoming obvious that the same congress was in place during the last six years and it wasn't all the fault of a previous administration.

You are starting to realize if it hadn't been for the previous administration the entrenched would have had this runaway six years ago. You hear the voice. You may not yet be willing to swallow your pride and admit unknown change was not a good idea, but the voice is speaking to you.

It's OK to make mistakes. Forgive yourself and move on to reverse what is happening.

It won't take many people to wake up and come alive to change the future of America for all time. Fifty-three percent of the voters in American voted for the change you are getting now. That is not much over 50%.

Only 5 to 10% of **WE THE PEOPLE** need to wake up and take aggressive, positive and immediate action to reverse this. Removing all the entrenched who are up for reelection in 2010 will be a beginning.

Follow that up with a new President as outlined in the chapter "The President" and the insanity will end, and responsible office holders can put on the brakes and stop this accelerating Stimulus Tragedy. Work can then begin to become responsible spenders and to lower taxes.

No longer can Americans blame the problems of the country on current presidents or past presidents.

No longer can Americans blame the problems of the country on present or past congresses.

No longer can Americans blame the problems of the country on business.

As stockholders of business the individual stockholder is responsible for the management of that business; in fact you own that business and are thereby responsible for the management of it.

As the purchaser of a home you are responsible for paying the mortgage. No one forced you to sign the mortgage or second mortgage or to pay too much for the home.

Any blame to be handed out belongs solely to **WE THE PEOPLE**. Every individual in America is responsible over and above all else.

WE THE PEOPLE elect congresses and presidents.

It is hypocrisy for you as an individual to blame anything on anyone other than yourself. Get over it and take responsibility.

Under the rights and privileges granted to every individual under the Constitution, we as individuals have the right and responsibility to be accountable for our decisions and actions.
WE THE PEOPLE are ultimately responsible for all of it.

The future will be whatever **WE THE PEOPLE** choose to make it.

"Where there is no vision, there is no hope."

George Washington Carver

Chapter 32

The Hope

WE THE PEOPLE have the ability and the responsibility to stop the Stimulus Tragedy. There is hope. The greatest hope lies in the Constitution.

Within the Constitution is the means to stop any process, even this one. Due process is written into the Constitution for a reason. When due process is followed as intended, the entire process works and works well.

When the due process of the Constitution is subverted, as is being done now, the process fails. Failure is unacceptable.

All that needs to happen is for the entrenched to be removed from office and due process will begin to be followed.

Hope resides in common sense. When common sense is allowed to be a part of the process the process works. It is important for Americans to move forward in a spirit of hope.

There is tremendous hope in this.

WE THE PEOPLE cannot allow partisan politics to dominate the process and expect to recover from this debacle. Since it is ultimately the responsibility of each individual American what the final result of the present insanity is to be, every American must be an active voice in recovery.

The hope is the Constitution. The hope is the individual. The hope is that common sense people make common sense decisions. The hope is that good people do good things in the best interest of America.

Hope comes in the knowing that when the entrenched are removed, a new President is elected and the principles of this book are implemented a reversal will be rapid and positive.

Economic recovery will be rapid and substantial within weeks of taking these actions. Confidence will be restored by just the announcement of these implementations. Government can't create stimulus.

It must come from positive thought, optimism and hope. And that can only come from the individual. True stimulus will be generated the moment common sense becomes practice.

Hope is a state of mind. It is the responsibility of every American to maintain hope. Every American must make up their mind a reversal is possible. Aggressive, positive and immediate action generates hope.

The solution then, is **WE THE PEOPLE** must do all we can do.

"Do not separate text from historical background. If you do, you will have perverted and subverted the Constitution, which can only end in a distorted, bastardized form of illegitimate government."

James Madison

Chapter 33

In Summary

Keep the faith! Keep the faith in the Constitution, the individual, the family, the worker, in small business, in America, in due process and in **WE THE PEOPLE**.

Don't allow these entrenched free spenders to destroy our future. Become involved and take aggressive, positive and immediate action.

Don't believe for one second the lie that free spending and bigger government are the answer.

The Constitution and **WE THE PEOPLE** are the only answer.

Economies are built from the bottom up, never from the top down.

That is why the founders of this great country put all the checks and balances into the Constitution. Remember, all the founders were subjects of a king. They understood the necessity of checks and balances.

The strength of America resides in the hands of **WE THE PEOPLE** as defined and protected by the Constitution.

America must protect and preserve these principles at all costs. Any subversion of due process is unconstitutional. America must not allow the entrenched to continue to subvert due process.

The life blood of America is the individual. This life blood is exemplified through the family, the worker and small business.

We are the driving force of America, not government. Government is of the people and for the people, not the other way around. Government was created as a necessary evil to serve the people.

The individual is not to be subjected to or to be made into indentured servants of government. Don't allow the entrenched, career, free spending politicians to dilute our freedoms or make us indentured servants with excessive taxes.

Americans don't need all these government programs.

Don't allow the entrenched to enact laws that will force us to pay excessive taxes.

When **WE THE PEOPLE** have the freedom to innovate and produce there is no need for government programs. America can be as great as it chooses to be if government stays out of the way. It's up to us to see they do.

The idea the entrenched are always trying to impress upon us is government is a business. This is a lie.

Government is inherently inefficient and dishonest. It is a bureaucracy and bureaucracy is always inefficient and dysfunctional.

There is presently no accountability in America's government. The entrenched are spending us into multi-generational debt and legislating us into socialism. Vote out the entrenched, elect a new President and reverse this, NOW!

There has never been a greater country on earth than the United States of America.

Citizens have the right to live, work and travel anywhere within it, unrestricted.

There are no limits in America for the individual.

Preserve and protect it at all costs! Fight for our freedom on all fronts!

"The man who reaches the right viewpoint and makes full consecration, and who fully idealizes himself as great, and who makes every act, however trivial, an expression of the ideal, has already attained to greatness. Everything he does will be done in a great way. He will make himself known, and will be recognized as a personality of power. He will receive knowledge by inspiration, and will know all that he needs to know. He will receive all the material wealth he forms in his thoughts, and will not lack for any good thing. He will be given ability to deal with any combination of circumstances which may arise, and his growth and progress will be continuous and rapid. Great works will seek him out, and all men will delight to do him honor."

**The Science of Being Great
Wallace D. Wattles**

Chapter 34

Be All You Can Be!

The personal ideals of the author are to preserve and defend the United States of America and help every other person be all they can be.

Be kind to yourselves. Feed your mind positively and nurture your inner self with positive, inspiring ideas and knowledge. Search out those people, ideas, books and activities that inspire and excite you.

Be proud to live in the greatest country in the history of the world. Be excited about it and let everyone know it. Defend America in all you think, say and do.

Believe and know that every American has the right and ability to be all they make up their mind to be. Set high, honorable and ambitious goals and work towards their attainment at all times. Look upon all people with compassion and hope.

Study the Declaration of Independence, the Constitution and Bill of Rights and feel the magnificence of each. Be proud and grateful they are yours as an individual. Study the history of each document and understand the personal sacrifices and risks that went into each of them.

Take that knowledge out into the world and protect and defend those principles at all costs.

America belongs to **WE THE PEOPLE,** and that is you!

Books and Resources

Tough Times Never Last, But Tough People Do!
Dr. Robert H. Schuller
http://www.crystalcathedral.org/

The Science of Being Great
Wallace D. Wattles

The Secret
Rhonda Byrne
Book and Movie
www.thesecret.tv

The Power of Your Subconscious Mind
Dr. Joseph Murphy

The Science of Being Rich
Wallace D. Wattles

The Master Key System
Charles Haanel
www.thesecret.tv

The Bible

My Utmost for His Highest
Oswald Chambers

All works of Emmet Fox

Hidden Power
James K. Van Fleet

Your Infinite Power to be Rich
Dr. Joseph Murphy

Political Information and Books

The 5000 Year Leap
W. Cleon Skousen
http://www.nccs.net/ftyl.html

The Heritage Foundation
http://www.heritage.org/

Congressmen by Length of Tenure
http://en.wikipedia.org/wiki/List_of_United_States_Co
ngressmen_by_longevity_of_service

Senators Tenure
http://wikibin.org/articles/us-senators-average-tenure-
increasing.html

Benefits of Senators
http://wiki.answers.com/Q/What_benefits_do_U.S._se
nators_receive

Rasmussen Reports Polling
www.rasmussenreports.com

The Dark Side of Illegal Immigration
http://www.usillegalaliens.com/

Federation for American Immigration Reform
http://www.fairus.org/site/PageServer?pagename=iic_i
mmigrationissuecentersf134

Federal Tax Brackets
http://www.moneychimp.com/features/tax_brackets.ht
m

Line Item Veto Act of 1996
http://en.wikipedia.org/wiki/Line_Item_Veto_Act_of_1
996

Second Amendment
http://en.wikipedia.org/wiki/Second_Amendment_to_t
he_United_States_Constitution

Tax Payers for Common Sense
http://www.taxpayer.net/

Charlie Reese
545 People Responsible For All of U. S. Woes
http://www.informationclearinghouse.info/article18568.
htm

What is a trillion dollars?
http://100777.com/node/455

How to Understand a Trillion-Dollar Deficit
By Barbara Kiviat
http://www.time.com/time/business/article/0,8599,187
0699,00.html

The Only Number You Need to Know
Mark Lieberman, Senior Economist
from FOXBusiness.com
http://www.foxbusiness.com/story/markets/number-
need-know/

The Stimulus Tragedy Blog
http://stimulustragedy.blogspot.com/

www.ingramcontent.com/pod-product-compliance
Lightning Source LLC
Chambersburg PA
CBHW061408280526
45784CB00001B/406